Anthony Wilson Thorold

On money

Anthony Wilson Thorold

On money

ISBN/EAN: 9783744722872

Printed in Europe, USA, Canada, Australia, Japan

Cover: Foto ©Suzi / pixelio.de

More available books at **www.hansebooks.com**

ON MONEY

BY

ANTHONY W. THOROLD D.D.
LATE LORD BISHOP OF WINCHESTER

NEW YORK
DODD, MEAD AND COMPANY
1896

ON MONEY

"THE SILVER IS MINE, AND THE GOLD IS MINE,
SAITH THE LORD OF HOSTS."

IT has been truly said by Sir Henry
Taylor, that there are few things in
the world of greater importance than
money. To despise it is an affectation
of virtue, and to ignore it is a confession
of folly.

See what it can do ! To the bulk of
mankind it is the focus of interest, at
once the stimulus of effort, and the
instrument of power. In a real and
intelligible sense it buys food, heals
disease, builds houses, prints books,
imparts knowledge, spreads education,
moves armies, augments happiness,
humanises life, promotes religion. If

it is not an end, it is certainly a means to an end. In every condition of life, and in all the circumstances of it, we are perpetually handling and using it for one purpose or another. The temptations to which it exposes us, the sacrifices to which it invites us, the good or the harm for which it enables us, on the one hand, help us to see why God gave Solomon riches as a special mark of favour ; on the other, to understand how St. Paul could write of it, " The love of money is the root of all evil" (1 Tim. vi. 6).

To use money we must possess it ; and whether we inherit it from others, or acquire it by our own exertion, it is equally a gift from God, and a trust for us.

Any one can see that in making money the conscience is incessantly confronted with the eternal inevitable laws of justice and truth. The exact line of demarcation betwéen right and wrong is always invisible ; but those who have most felt the difficulty of finding it for their own guidance are also most likely to be indulgent to the difficulties of their neighbours. So, when we hear a surprise expressed that Christian people can be found to justify either the manufacture or the sale of such articles of consumption as human infirmity converts to purposes of sin, will not a kindly common sense bid them go a little farther back in the problem, and ask how ever it could please a good and just God to create the hop and the vine? There can, however, be no doubt at all that use and habit do blunt the edge of conscience, and that self-interest, when stimulated by a love of gain, closely shuts the eye to the moral of the case and thus blinds it to the harm.

Several other points, however, less palpable, but quite as important, soon turn up in the intricate, but interesting casuistry of this part of the subject. Is it possible to make too much money?

Is speculation lawful? To what extent, and on what grounds, are we justified in praying for commercial success ?

A certain degree of accumulation seems consistent with that instinct of wise forethought which, like our other instincts, we may reasonably conceive to have been implanted in us for legitimate indulgence. When St. Paul appeals to the habit of mankind, in parents laying up for children rather than children for parents, as a ground for his own unwillingness to be burdensome to the Church, his recognition of the practice is tantamount to an approval of it. It is not only reasonable, but praiseworthy, that the head of a family should by diligence and frugality be in a position to spare his widow, at the moment when she has care and grief enough in other ways, the additional anxiety of a sudden poverty; to give his sons enough to start them with in their professions, and to send his daughters not quite empty-handed from their father's house to their husbands'. The hardest life and much quiet self-denial are unspeakably sweetened to a manly and generous nature by the thought that when the heads and hands that have so steadily worked for others are becoming dust in the ground, the love that nerved to that work, and made it pleasanter than any selfish indulgence, will have secured its reward.

But it is quite another thing for a Christian deliberately to make his life one long grind in a counting-house, and to turn not only his youth, but even his later years, into a perpetual slavery, only to swell his personal possessions, and, perhaps, to point in his own case the Saviour's mournful warning—" Woe unto you who are rich, for ye have received your consolation " (Luke vi. 24).

Of course, political economy will treat any hint like this with un-

disguised contempt, and sufficiency
is a very relative word; and few young
men have sense enough to prefer to
make their fortune for themselves; and
what in past and simpler days would
have been called a competent, though
modest, dowry for an English gentle-
woman, might now hardly suffice to
supply her with clothes.   Still, wealth
with all its subtle joys and sense of
power is a great snare and peril.   To
hundreds and thousands of us covetousness *is* idolatry, for we put our
money in the place of God to us, when
we treat it as our consolation and
security—the source of our dignity,
the weapon of our defence.   Yet it is
a poor god to worship, when it takes
all the leisure from the life, all the
comfort from the home, all the bright-
ness from the face, all the nobleness
from the character.   If you succeed, it
is at the loss both of the sweetness
and repose that are the true charms of
human existence; if you fail, you lose

both worlds. Thus it is that to the
man who fears God and values his
own consistency, and understands
something of human nature, and steadily looks on into the other world, the
question, sooner or later, will and
must occur, "Is not the time come
that I have enough; and shall not I
better please God, and help my own
salvation by retiring from the anxie-
ties of my career?" Or, if such may
not be, and it does sometimes happen
that the entire relinquishment of active employment has a serious if not
fatal result, a good man may easily
resolve with himself that the occupa-
tion he will continue for his health's
sake, but henceforward the profit of it
shall be for God.

Yet there is one noble justification
for that plodding and almost insatiable
pursuit of wealth that so markedly
characterises modern Englishmen. I
mean the secret resolute aim of accom-
plishing, single-handed, some blessed

Christian enterprise that shall live after us, and work by us, long after the silver and gold we have acquired have passed to our heirs. There are many among us who have done this; many more who are capable of it if it were pressed home to their consciences as a duty for God.

What was the real, the beautiful secret of that passionate love of poverty wnicn, with all tne self-love that spoiled it, and the small extravagances that disfigured it, was still such a moral force in the Middle Ages, when the Church had all but forgotten how to overcome the world? Was it not in this, that it was endured for Christ's sake, as a means of resembling and honouring Him?

Why cannot we be content also to be rich for Christ's sake, and to try to say, in the deepest sense of the word, "I have learned both to be full and to be hungry, both to abound and to suffer need?" (Phil. iv. 12). There are hundreds and thousands of wealthy men and women in England at this moment not only making a Christian profession, but eminently worthy of it, who simply, from want of direction, are blind to their opportunities for glorifying God through the wealth lying idle in their hands. They have ample for their heirs, and for their own needs, and for the decorous conventional charities that society expects of them—ample, also, for some individual act of useful, practical, permanent munificence, which might be their vase of ointment for the head of their blessed Lord, fragrant and honourable till He comes back in His glory. Yes, each Christian to whom the blessed opportunity is given—and many more possess it than care to know—should resolve to leave behind some mark of real self-denial, to be his monument when he is gone. A church, a school, a bed in a hospital, a mission-house, the support of a mis-

sionary : let us choose what we please,
only let us do something. The more
sacrifice it involves, the more precious
in Christ's sight will the offering be.
" She hath done what she could "
(Mark xiv. 8). How few since Mary's
day have earned that praise !

In trying to think out the abstract
lawfulness of speculation, the first
thing to make clear is what speculation means ; for there are two very
different things expressed by the same
word. If we simply mean by it the
bold and prompt seizing of an opportunity, through the clear foresight that
guesses the turn of the market, or the
practised skill that calculates how the
events of the day will affect exchange,
then it is but the legitimate exercise
of a special and valuable kind of
talent. The welfare of society is often
greatly promoted by the happy ven-
tures of commercial enterprise ; and to
forbid such efforts would be but a
feeble and silly attempt to paralyse

the energy and to impede the progress of mankind.

But where speculation is a mere gambling throw in the dark, the rash impulse of a lazy and ignorant hardihood to make in a week what honest work could barely make in a year; imperilling precious interests on the chance of a die, and fostering in the character just those instincts and tendencies that make industry intolerable, and tempt men to exchange the serious business of life for the risks of a lottery, the individual speculator not only injures himself, but he defrauds the community. He injures himself, for he can never enjoy that real sweetness of success with which honest labour sooner or later rewards us; he defrauds the community, since it does not receive from him that contribution of diligent and useful production which is wanted to augment the general capital of the State.

To a Christian mind one key to the

difficulty may be found in that practice
of asking God's blessing on any pro-
posed enterprise, which is the habit of
those who fear God.

There are clearly two distinct lines
of thought in which prayer about temporal blessings may be conceived to
run. There is the prayer for divine
guidance as to the *lawfulness* of any
particular scheme under consideration.
"Will God approve my doing this?"
There is also the prayer *for divine
blessing* on the scheme, when the de-
cision has been made. "May God
prosper this now that it is to be
done!" It is certain that if good men
were more careful to ask for counsel
on the propriety of any particular
enterprise before making up their
minds to it, instead of first deciding,
and then asking for success, many
mistakes would be avoided, and much
distress saved.

A man, with wife and children, has
five thousand pounds at his disposal,

which he has put out at moderate
interest on valid security. One day
he sees a prospectus of a railway
across Honduras, or, perhaps, a Japan
loan, which would pay him fifteen per
cent. His imagination is fired. He
appreciates with a vivid and perilous
facility the comforts that could be procured, and, perhaps, the money put
by, with so much additional income.
He cannot see anything wrong in
doing the best he can for himself;
really, there is hardly anything to ask
about. He makes up his mind, acts,
then prays to be prospered, and waits
the result of his venture, fortified by
the delusive consciousness of having
implored the blessing of God. But
had he first of all asked to be guided
as to the expediency, as well as the
lawfulness, of the step he was propos-
ing, He who gives "wisdom to all
men" might have helped him to see
that the augmented income, plus the
risk, the anxiety, the feverishness of

B

mind about money engendered by such transactions in ordinary natures, and the love of it for its own sake so easily fostered by any temporary success, do not counterbalance the smaller income and the surer investment, and the un-broken tranquillity. The "still small voice" might have said, 'Leave it alone : they that will be rich fall into temptation and a snare.' Trust me" (1 Tim. vi. 9).

But, assuming that our enterprise is lawful, and that we are justifiably con-fident of the divine sanction on our undertakings, there still remains a question of moment for those who, just because they so fully believe in prayer, desire to pray reasonably and according to the will of God. Can it be right directly to ask God to prosper our efforts—which in some cases may amount to a request for ten thousand pounds ? or is it better to confine our-selves simply to laying the matter before Him, in the simple confidence

of loyal children who wish to tell Him
everything, knowing that He will bless
us in this way or in that (without our
direct asking), as He may see it to be
for our good? The question is complicated by many considerations; and
every man must have liberty of conscience about it. The writer's own
conviction, however, is clear, that
while in spiritual things we should
both ask and trust, for there we can
have no doubt about the good of what
we ask for, in temporal things (beyond
actual necessities), after having poured
out our heart before God, we should
trust and not ask.

For temporal things, up to a certain
point, we are indeed both permitted
and commanded to pray. " Give us
this day our daily bread " (Matt. vi. 1)
is a petition of our Saviour's own
dictating, and, though one man's daily
bread may mean something very different from another man's ; and it is
not safe to trust every one with the

definition of what the necessaries of life may be, there is nevertheless a distinction both reasonable and intelligible, between the prayer that asks God according to His promise to supply our necessities, and the prayer that asks of Him to pour vast wealth into our lap. Our modern society is in such a state of mutual interdependence and entanglement, that often for me to gain, my neighbour must lose ; and so the event that enriches me, improverishes him. Then, though it may be good for one man suddenly to step into a position of affluence, it may be ruinous for another man ; and God, loving the two men equally, will, just because of that love, in one case bestow, in the other deny.

Material prosperity, so far from being the highest good, is in itself neither good nor evil ; but it will turn to good or evil, according to the character with which it is brought in contact, and the spirit in which it is met and

used.   Surely a thoughtful parent
would pause and muse, before out of
a choice of blessings at his disposal
for some beloved child he decided on
the gift of great riches.   May we not
reverently suppose that thoughts of
this kind pass through the heart of
our heavenly Father as He looks
round on us; and is not there wisdom
in the self-control that refuses to press
Him for a gift, which may be health,
and may be poison ?

For nothing tries a man more than
the sudden loss or gain of money.
The loss of it, while it goads some
men to an amazing and almost noble
effort to recover it, will so sour and
paralyse others, that henceforth they
cease to be capable of further struggle
with the world.   The gain of it is
good for some, is perhaps worse for
more.   Men who, while enjoying a
modest competency, have been simple,
kind, and charitable, have found in a
great accession of wealth an instant

occasion for a sordid and wretched meanness. A sudden rush of selfishness will sometimes flood the heart that thinks itself permanently raised over the necessities of friendship, or even the protection of Providence. Summer time parches the soil as well as ripens the harvest; and to need man's sympathy is a great help to giving it.

If the first thing about money is to get it, the second is to keep it. And it is not so easy to keep it. Most people have some sort of screw loose in their private money matters. Either they invest it foolishly, or they spend it wastefully ; or, what is almost the worst possible thing to do with it, they hoard it covetously ; and either way, it is their Lord's money hidden down in the earth, instead of being put out to use for Him.

The investment of money is just one of those questions which it is real wisdom to think over very carefully,

till our mind is made up about it;
and then, when once settled, it should
be put away upon a shelf, to be left
there. Money, like every other talent,
is to be made the most of; and it is
our duty to see that we do make the
most of it, or it is worth just so much
less, both for our own use, and our
power of sharing it with others. But
making the most of it does not necessarily mean getting the highest
possible return for it; simply, the
highest interest compatible with good
security.

Now it is quite true that to be able
to have all one's property invested in
land, or consols, there had better be
a great deal of it; and that the difference between three per cent. and six
per cent. will often mean to the strug-
gling father of a large family the salary
of a governess, or a boy's schooling, or
the summer holiday, or the annual
premium on his life insurance. Still, the
old duke's maxim that "high interest

means bad security" is a perfectly sound one. A little more income for ten years, at the cost of losing all for ever afterwards, is a poor bargain; and an assured, if smaller, income has a rest and a comfort about it that, to a dabbler in foreign bonds, or speculative railways, is often an object of profound envy.

It is an old proverb, "never to carry all your eggs in the same basket;" and if your fortune is invested in more securities than one, it must be a storm indeed that robs you of everything. Usually a house, if judiciously chosen, is a sensible investment. It is natural to prefer to be one's own landlord. To be living under a roof that belongs to us is not only to live at less rent; but it permits us to drive a nail into the wall, or to throw two rooms into one without an uneasy dread of the landlord's displeasure. For country people, it unquestionably gives an interest to life to watch the trees grow up that your hands have planted ; and year by year to make fresh improvements in what you can bequeath to others, more beautiful and more valuable than when it first became your own.

After all, as we have said already, the great aim should be to do the best we can in putting out our money, that we may be saved all anxiety about it afterwards. Very few persons out of business life can be safely trusted to make their own investments. It is money well spent to procure the best advice on the subject ; and it is true economy when the advice is given, to take it. Fidgetiness often leads to covetousness ; perpetually to be fancying that we are on the point of being ruined, or that we are making less interest than we might make if we managed more cleverly, deteriorates the character, and robs the life of peace. Greediness for a higher income often brings its wholesome

punishment by an eventual loss both
of capital and income.

If the first thing about money is to
get it, and the second to keep it, the
third is to use it. And this, perhaps,
needs the greatest wisdon of all. Remember what it implies, and what it
includes. It implies foresight, so as
to be ready for losses ; self-control, to
be able to go without things that we
should vastly like, but cannot afford ;
patience, to know how to wait for
what we wish for ; discretion, clearly
to perceive what will suit us best ;
self-denial, that we may help others ;
conscientiousness, that in all we spend
we may please God ; good sense, to
draw the right line between extremes
on either side ; a joyous liberty of
heart, to trust the kindness of God,
that He means us to be happy. If
not to offend in word is one sign of
perfection, to make a right use of
money is another. It is significant
that Dives went to his trouble, not for

viciousness, but for self-indulgence. It was the snare of his great posses-sions that stole from Christ the soul of the rich young man, whom to see was to love.

See, too, what it includes. Certainly three things ; some would say four. There is maintenance, and usefulness, and enjoyment, and—may we not add ? —saving. Each of these has its own natural order ; each its own relation and proportion to all the rest.

Clearly we must live : in other words, we must eat and drink, and wear clothes, and live under shelter— the needs, it may be said, even of savages. But our artificial and civilised life makes other demands on us still. There are children to educate ; ser-vants to feed and pay ; now and then doctor's bills ; occasionally lawyers' ; and for the absolutely needful claims of a middle-class English household, with its varied and complicated and incessant expenditure, the one word maintenance means a heavy drain of money. By usefulness, I mean that proportion of money which, before any other expenditure is incurred, next after our maintenance, should deliberately, methodically, and cheerfully, be put by for God. Enjoyment will include all that personal expense which, within just limits, and according to the discretion of the individual conscience is a legitimate source of human joy. Saving or putting by, either in the shape of a life insurance, or in the private laying up of a certain amount of income for sickness or old age, will be, in the judgment of many, a prudent, if rather an Irish way of using by keeping.

Few things require more pains, show more character, or earn more results, than the expenditure of money for household necessities. Several points strike one here as indisputable, but singular. How much more some people spend on mere eating and drinking than others. How this is true, not only of navvies, and pitmen, and artisans, but of persons of all ranks and circumstances. How apt such persons are to complain of their poverty, and that they never have money for anything else. How easily such luxuries come to be looked upon as the indispensable necessaries of life. How the simpler and more frugal people, who would equally like them, but go without them, because other things seem to come first, never get credit for their thriftiness but are assumed not to mind about them. How little any one gets for his money spent this way, except dyspepsia and a habit of self-indulgence. How quite the worst and silliest way of spending money is to eat and drink it.

But our household expenditure means other possibilities of extravagance than those of food. Costly changes in furniture, not for being worn out, but for being old-fashioned ;

what is called "stylish living," so often the pretentious vulgarity of pseudo gentle-people, and so miserably and deservedly failing in procuring the consideration it spends so much to buy; an expensive way of entertaining, which gratifies nobody but the tradesmen who supply the goods; servants simply to minister to laziness: and incessant going to and fro to this place or that, merely because home is dull: these are items of expense which swell the house-bills of many a quiet family, with little in return but constant mortification, and the pressure of debt.

The plain truth is, and there is much consolation it it, that the actual necessaries of life form a much less item in household expenditure than many of us are willing to suppose: that it is the extras, and the luxuries, and the superfluities that run away with the money; that the sooner a somewhat stern and decided check is put on modern habits of spending, the better it will be for all of us ; and that if the recent rise in prices helps to affect a little household economy, and compels some of us to ask ourselves if we could not be quite as well and as happy with cheaper and simpler ways, the country would be wealthier through its increased savings, and in many homes the purse at the end of the year would be much fuller than now.

In quite their proper place clothes have a claim for consideration among the other items of domestic spending ; and though the present age hardly needs encouragement in this direction, it is a real mistake to treat them as a matter of indifference. Whatever is worth doing at all is worth doing well ; and it is by no means an open question whether clothes are to be worn. The right thing to do is to spend just that amount of attention and money on them that in the end will prove the true

economy. To care nothing for dress
is, indeed, not quite such a snare as to
care too much for it. It is no exaggera-
tion to say that costliness of wardrobe
is one of the glaring inconsistencies of
our modern Christianity; and makes
shrewd men and women of the world
coldly and scornfully ask, where is the
cross that such Christians carry. Yet
when God gives any one personal
attractions, He entrusts them with a
means of influence which He expects
to be made use of; and there are two
kinds of vanity, that which affects to
despise natural gifts, and that which
assumes a personal pre-eminence from
them. But be there beauty or no, it is
still reasonable and natural to wish to
make the best of ourselves. For we
should dress, not only for our own
fancy, but to please those we live with.
A true wife likes to please her husband's
eye; and a father is gratified by seeing
his daughters dress as suits him. But
clothes cost money; and while extremes

on both sides should be carefully avoided, quite the most wasteful plan is to give it no thought at all. "Can a maid forget her ornaments?" (Jeremiah ii. 32) is an inspired question, which has its root in the intrinsic reasonableness of some kind of care being given to them ; and the elevated temperament that treats clothes and their cognate subjects with a lofty negligence is certain to be extravagant, and likely to be shabby.

The right spending of money also includes usefulness. And I choose this word in preference to charity, because it contains and expresses more. A Christian's hourly conviction about all his spending should be that he is a steward for God, both as regards himself and his neighbour. Among the rough tests of the genuineness of our religion, none is so sure as our habit of giving away.

But this is one of those matters in which the truest wisdom is to be at once methodical and free.   A conscientious man should, as a matter of course, set aside a certain part of his income as belonging to God, and sacredly to be dedicated to Him.   The principle, however, once recognised, the special application of it must vary according to the individual case.   Are there many children or few ?   Is the annual income professional and fluctuating, or permanent and certain ?   Here are, at least, two among other conditions which will materially affect the power, and so the duty of giving.   Such proportion inflexibly set aside for the Master's use need not necessarily be all that is given. Sometimes it may be more, though it never should be less.   If it fall short in one year it should be made up in another.   Any sudden accession of fortune, or great hit in worldly success, should be recognised by a special thank-offering ; gratefully, for it is He who gives us power to get wealth ; promptly, for the sooner it is done the more likely it is to be well done. A gift deferred often means a gift diminished. That it is set apart for divine uses does not necessarily imply that it should all be devoted to strictly religious purposes.

There are many doors into the Temple of Charity, and various are the altars on which our offering may be laid. Occasionally it is found a good rule to apportion the charity purse under the four divisions of religious, benevolent, domestic, and casual—part going regularly in annual subscriptions, part to collections in church, part to special objects such as occur annually with almost inconvenient regularity, part not assigned at all, but left free for the discretion of the hour. Only let us take care that our charity be not so mechanical as to lose all its true vitality, so much a matter of habit, that we forget, when we give, humbly to offer it to our God. It is the motive that makes the gift precious—in the grateful love that lays it at the Lord's feet once pierced to save us, in the wondering joy that thrills through the heart, that God should accept anything from our hands. Then, when God is remembered, and His poor cared for, and His kingdom promoted, and our own flesh and blood not coldly pushed aside, are we free, as conscience shall permit us and our means justify it, occasionally to think of our own wishes and gratify our own tastes. "Rather give alms of such things as ye have, and behold all things are clean unto you" (Luke xi. 41). When people ask if it can be consistent with simplicity and self-denial to buy a picture, or to own a carriage, or to take a tour, when all these things spend money that might be directly used for the glory of our Master, let us not fear to say, *it is*, if nothing else comes so near us as to make the indulgence unlawful. For two reasons. First, because one end of money is enjoyment ; and God gives it us, among other purposes, to minister

to this enjoyment; and He rejoices
over our joy in His gifts, as a tender
human parent is glad in his child's
gladness at some present of his own.
Oh, we do our heavenly Father wrong,
if we suppose that No is the word He
likes best to say to us. His is no
austere nature that can neither smile
nor bless; and if out of our superfluity
we would sometimes buy something
that to possess would please us, let us
ask His leave and be free.

Another reason is, that society, in all
the immense varieties of its complex
life, exists and grows by the mutual
interdependence of its members; that
He who has implanted in us the love
of art, or of music, or of books, or of
nature, or of travel, must intend and
sanction the moderate indulgence of
them; that the Christian, so far from
needing to feel himself debarred these
innocent recreations, should feel himself as free as other men for them; for
is it not a Father's world in which we

find ourselves, and are not these merci-
fully given us for happiness? He
who has wreathed the face with smiles,
and endowed us with the blessed
sense of humour, and given flowers
their odours, and made the outer
world so exceeding glorious, has
taught us, as in a parable, that our
joy is His joy, only let it always be
in Him.

There are, however, two things more
to say. It may be that at the moment
when we are meditating such indulgence, some pressing necessity, or out-
side sorrow, comes in, and a voice says
to us, " Canst thou cheerfully deny
thyself, and spare that money for me?"
At such a moment—and it will not
always, perhaps not often, come, God
is too kind, too just to overtask us—
let us lift up our heart for strength, and
then, looking once more at our coveted
treasure, for our Saviour's sake, bravely
let it go. The quiet happiness that
distils into the heart, when He smiles

on us His thanks, must be felt to be known.

Or, there may be those in whose heart, through the special and exceeding grace of the Holy Spirit, there is now an utter deadness and indifference to such things, not because there never was any natural inclination for them, but because the power of the new life has smothered it out. The extent of their indifference is the measure of their victory. Well, blessed are they in their utter contentment with their Lord, and in their joy in sacrifice. They are on a height, which no one can reach without much steep climbing, and some falls.

Lord Bacon, in his Essay on Expense, clearly points out that "he that is plentiful in expense of all kinds, will hardly be preserved from decay." While one hobby judiciously and moderately indulged, can hardly hurt a poor man, half a dozen may make a bankrupt of a rich one. That idiosyn-

crasies of expense have, on the whole,
been beneficial to society needs no
arguing; since but for the costly en-
thusiasm of private, and sometimes
eccentric collectors, there would be
none of those accumulations of art and
books and sculpture that give all classes
a share in the enjoyment of their
wealthier neighbours, and sow broad-
cast the fruitful seed of many a lofty
thought and noble production. This,
too, is certain, that pictures, plate,
marquettry, china, or vertu of any
kind, when really good of its sort, is a
valuable investment if you can wait for
your interest; to buy well, even if you
pay highly, is a safe protection against
ultimate loss. No doubt the difficulty,
however, that most men find in this
direction is knowing where to stop, for
every one can appreciate Dr. Johnson's
experience, that abstinence is easier
than temperance. Conscience has a
voice that claims to be heard about
every penny spent on self-indulgence;

and when sternly silenced, it waits for its revenge.

There are, however, two useful checks on our habits of expenditure, which, if not strictly to be called moral, yet tend that way, since they act as helps to the conscience, though not to be recognised as quite on a level with it. One of them is the habit of saving, the other the practice of keeping accounts. It is hardly too much to say about saving that it is a primary instinct of human nature, and that in proportion to the savings of a nation will be the increase of its wealth and independence and power. Englishmen are, with one exception, probably quite the least thrifty of civilised nations, and if some of us need convincing that it is important to save, still more refuse to admit that it is possible. Many persons, indeed, appear to regard thriftiness as identical with a certain meanness of disposition, and think that no one can save but at the cost of his

own dignity and his neighbour's interests, ·and the easy indulgence so generally granted to the selfish thought-
fulness of young spendthrifts indicates
a fallacy latent in the popular mind,
that any kind of waste is, on the whole,
for the public good. Now, is it quite
too bold to hazard two statements on
this subject : one, that most people
ought to save ; another, that a large
minority can ? That most people ought
to save is capable of proof, from the
standpoint both of self-interest and
religion. That every one can save—
obvious exceptions allowed for—is
plain from the fact that all of us waste
a certain amount every year on some
sort of superfluity, which, though spent
gradually and almost unconsciously,
and mostly in small sums, makes a
considerable total at the end of the
twelve months, and which, if not spent,
would have been still at our disposal.

The prudence of saving may almost
be called self-evident. Illness, mis-

fortune, the opportunity of an eligible
purchase, putting out children into the
world, the inevitable growth of expenditure as we advance in life, the
immense comfort of a secret provision
for emergencies, are quite sufficient in
themselves to justify and reward the
thrift that springs from self-denial,
apart from the distinct motive of laying
by for accumulation, which it may or
may not be right to do. Though it
may not tell directly upon our habits
of benevolence, and in many cases it
will not ; in quite as many more it will
tell indirectly, through promoting self-
restraint, and placing additional means
at our disposal. For if we are poor,
through what we miss as well as
through what we lose, we are rich
through what we save as much as
through what we gain. By all means
let us admit that the habit of saving
has a dangerous side to it ; that to
save merely to keep is quite a different
thing from saving that we may give

away; and that where pride, or
stinginess, or covetousness, is at the
bottom of it, it is but selfishness in
perhaps a more specious form. Nevertheless, much inconvenience would be
saved, and even greater distress avoided,
if it was felt to be a rule of common
prudence to lay by something yearly,
whether much or little, against an evil
day. No one can be rich who lives
beyond his income, and no one can be
poor who lives within it.

The habit of keeping accounts to
some people seems the only possible
way of saving themselves from waste
and debt, while others scoff at it as a
piece of useless pedantry. And it is
quite true that if the money is spent,
writing down in a book how it is
spent will not get it back again. It
is also true that for private individuals,
at the end of every year, at the risk of
their own temper and the comfort of
their family, and the loss of much
precious time, to insist on balancing

their accounts to a halfpenny, is a kind
of financial pedantry which (all respect
to Charles Simeon notwithstanding)
good sense will usually repudiate as
utterly needless. But admitting all
this, there is still real advantage in
the regular keeping of accounts which
is quite worth a certain amount of constant trouble, and which, if not pushed
to an extreme, is a valuable help to
conscientious persons. Writing down
the cost of something which, perhaps,
you did not really want, or ought not
to have paid such a high price for, may
give you a useful qualm of conscience
on being brought face to face with it,
and may prevent your repeating the
error. Those who are methodical
enough to apportion definite amounts
to the various items of their expenditure, and who would be honestly dis-
tressed if the allotment, say to personal
expenditure, was seriously augmented
to the injury of other claims, have an
easy way of ascertaining from their

private record how far they are fulfil-
ling their own intentions. Any one
who honestly feels that giving away
a certain proportion of his income is
a distinct and pressing duty will from
time to time be careful to ascertain
how far he is really giving in charity
a due proportion, as God prospers him.
But there is no readier way than that
of glancing over his account-book, and
finding there in the black and white of
his own handwriting how much he
has received and how much he has
given.

It belongs to this part of our subject
to observe how directly, and univer-
sally, and continually, and on the
whole reasonably, social opinion claims
to pronounce its verdict on the right
use a man makes of his money. The
question, "What is he worth?" may
often be asked with a purely worldly
meaning, and the answer given will
usually be, not that he is just, or pure,
or true, or kindly, or highly educated,

but that his income is so much a year.
There is also seen in some people an
impertinent curiosity about their neighbours' private affairs that cannot too
instantly or too sharply be snubbed.
Worldly-wise men will always show a
cautious reticence on this subject, and
some one in "Coningsby" is made to
say that the pleasant thing is to have
ten thousand a year, and to be supposed
to have only five. While, however, no
wise man will ever wish to be thought
richer than he is, an honest man will
hardly try to make it out that he is
poorer. Admitting what has been
already observed about unjustifiable
intrusion into other men's affairs,
there is still a kind of rough though
sometimes inconvenient reasonableness
in the anxiety of a man's neighbours
to discover what share he may fairly
be invited to take in the duties and
burdens of his neighbourhood. While
there is only too much disposition
among some Englishmen to be ob-

sequious to rich men, and to give a disproportionate influence to the possessor of wealth, it is on all accounts desirable to rouse in every one a real conviction of the responsibility of possessing it. Never should it be forgotten that the daily tribunal of public opinion, before which every one of us, consciously or unconsciously, willingly or unwillingly, is compelled to stand, is but the faint type and precursor of that final judgment-seat before which the rich and poor will some day meet together, and from which One who has Himself been poor will judge His brethren without respect of persons.

It is probably the presentiment of this tribunal that induces many worldly persons at the last moment to attempt to atone at their death for the shortcomings of their life by giving their money away when they can no longer keep it for their own purposes, and, perhaps to the injury of their own flesh and blood, to leave the world with a flourish of trumpets in the shape of ostentatious legacies to charitable institutions, for which, when living, they neither thought nor cared. Such gifts can neither bribe God nor deceive men. When, however, they fitly conclude a life of consistent benevolence, they are the becoming farewell of a Christian's heart to the world he is leaving, whose woes he can no longer heal. And this brings us to a part of our subject which it is impossible to pass over without some consideration—the right disposition of money after we are dead by what is called a will.

Superstition with some persons, indolence with others, indecision or changeableness with others, will often cause men to postpone to an inconvenient or hurried moment what, for the sake of others as well as themselves, should be done when the health is strong, the judgment clear, the leisure sufficient, and the will unbiassed. It is quite true that in some

cases the law makes a man's will for
him, even better than he could make it
for himself; and that, unless he is
able to keep his own counsel about it,
the risk of disappointing those whose
expectations he has excited may
seriously affect his freedom of action
if he wishes to change his mind. It is
equally true that the absence of a will
is often productive not only of great
inconvenience but also of wretched
discord; and at a moment when a profound sorrow might be expected to
bind together brothers and sisters by
the sad tie of a common sympathy,
they leave their father's grave to
plunge into a miserable strife for the
wealth he has left behind. It is a
serious question how far, in making
their wills, people are sufficiently
aware of the life-long resentments that
so often follow them; or, on the other
hand, of the grateful kindliness which
the tender mention of a name, or the
bequeathing of some trifling legacy,

can stir in the heart that rejoices to feel itself loved. Injustice in a will rankles and cankers in the wounded memory for a whole lifetime. To be cut off with a shilling is a kind of malignant insult, now happily falling into general disuse; and, as a rule, the shorter wills are, the fewer complications they involve afterwards; but to be totally passed over in the will of one quite near to you, without your name being mentioned, is sometimes quite as vexatious to a sensitive heart. Our last thoughts of those we love should be tender thoughts; and it helps us to remember them, to know that they remembered us.

Among the practical lessons which a careful parent will constantly inculcate upon his children, and the pithy maxims that will be falling from his lips, almost without his knowing them, none can be more important in their nature, more incessant in their influence, or more permanent in their re-

sult, than those which bear upon
money. It is easy to make too much
of it, and it is possible to make too
little.

Where the one aim of the head of a
family is plainly seen to be to become
rich ; and when the constant burden of
his talk is on the power and importance
of money ; his children will inevitably
be trained for their father's Mammon-
worship, and the air of filthy lucre
they daily breathe will insensibly im-
pregnate their moral character. If, on
the other hand, they see money treated
as a matter of utter indifference ; if
before their eyes day by day expenses
are incurred without means to meet
them, and the last question ever asked
about anything is what it will cost,
there will be a tendency in the other
direction to impair the quickness of
the moral sense in money matters
generally, habitual self-indulgence will
seem to be the natural order of things,
and to wish for anything, will mean

instantly to try to procure it. No
doubt in many persons there are what
may be called hereditary ideas about
money: some are born frugal, others
extravagant; and be the circumstances
of life what they may, the original bias
will assert itself from the nursery to
the grave. But a great deal may be
done by carefully educating children
in the true value of money as means
to an end. There are various ways of
doing it, and some of them will at first
be disappointing. Different characters
must be differently treated, and an age,
which might be suitable for one young
person to be trusted with money,
might be very unsuitable for another.
You begin to give your boy an allowance, with much good advice on the
right way of spending it; and you are
mortified, when he returns for his first
vacation to find that you have to pay
your money twice over. His allowance is all spent—he really does not
know how—and the bills, which it

ought to have paid, are sent home to
you. Well, give him a sharp scold-
ing; be sure not to let him think you
feel him capable of having wilfully de-
ceived you; cheerfully trust him again,
and the chances are it is the last time
it will happen. If it is good for lads
to be gradually trained to the use of
money, it is quite as important for
girls. Not only is it an additional interest in their life; but it prepares
them for the time when they will have
to keep house for a husband or a
brother; and it is a constant opportunity of secret self-denial to devout
hearts, that love to spare what they
can for God.

The chief thing, however, that wise
parents should din into their children's
memory, and impress on their consciences almost from the first hour
they are capable of understanding it,
is the misery, and bondage, and even
disgrace that come with debt. Borrowing seems so easy, and lending so

natural, and youth is buoyant with hope, and conscious of integrity. " It is only for a short time, and payment will easily be made; and who need know ? " But a tendency of this kind should be burned out of a young man's nature as with a hot iron. It is a fault towards which an inflexible sternness is at once the kindest, and the only effective remedy. An indulgent easiness in the early days of youth may foster a habit which will paralyse the sinews of robust action, and reduce ultimately its victim to the contemptible condition of being either a mendicant or a thief. If the earliest commission of a fault of this kind is severely punished; at the moment, the first fault may be the last; while one condoned offence may be, not only to the offender, but to all the rest of the family, a false symptom of parental weakness, that may result in a harvest of sorrow. It is true that if no one would lend, no one could borrow.

But not all lending is to pay debts, and not all borrowing is to discharge them. As a rule, it is sometimes much better, where there is a claim of blood or friendship on you, to give half rather than lend all. Where there is delicacy of feeling the request is not likely to be repeated from the same quarter, and often you are as happy to aid, as your friend to be aided. There will often also be cases where, from the conviction that the granting of a loan would be mischievous or useless, for very friendship's sake, painful though it be, it is our duty firmly to say No.

But lending as a rule from friend to friend or relative to relative is sometimes a very hazardous proceeding on one side, if not on both ; for the time of repaying is never quite convenient, and a borrower's memory is often treacherous. It is a cynic's remark, founded on painful experience of average human nature, that to get rid of a

man you don't want, the shortest way
is to lend him money.

A dry and somewhat dull subject is
now drawing to its close ; and it is not
easy to light it up either with the gleams
of fancy or the touches of feeling that
float other topics on a reader's sympa-
thies. There are still, however, two
points of view, in which it may be
usefully considered for the benefit of
those who have but little of it, and for
the study of all who have yet to be
convinced that, be it much or little, it
never leaves us as it finds us ; it makes
us worse or better.

One of the wisest and kindest of our
living authors has said, " How happy
life can be with plenty of employment
and very little money ; " and his words
will perhaps more easily find acceptance
with those who have made their money,
than those who have it yet to make.
It will, however, seem less of a paradox,
if we limit its application mainly to that
period of life when the character is full

of energy, the body active with vital
power, and when the exquisite and
unsated instincts of enjoyment find an
ever-varied scope in pursuits and en-
gagements to which advanced life is
unequal. But, paradox or not, it is
true. In the increase of wealth there
is ever an increase of worry. Your
money must be invested, and you
cannot easily decide as to the right way
of doing the best with it. Or you make
costly purchases, which often want
more looking after than you ever
bargained for. The more you buy the
more the margin of your cares is increased, the more numerous are the
hostages that you give to fortune. You
can't lose what you don't possess.
Burglars will not steal your simple
plate, which they never suspect to be
silver; no one cheats you with the
horses you do not wish to buy; you
are saved perhaps a week's vexation
by never being outbidden for a picture
which you had resolved on securing;

the storm that sweeps down the lofty
forest trees spares the humble shrubs
that clasp the hill.

To have just enough, and to know
that it is enough, and to be thankful for
it—this is the secret which the Gospel
long ago proclaimed to mankind, but
which the wisdom of this world rejects
with scorn. Yet to suppose that a
modest competence, such as modern
times would call utter poverty, has no
real charms or vivid enjoyments of its
own, is a profound mistake. It is full
of joy, though of the simplest and
purest kind. Let some of us middle-
aged people who, after twenty or thirty
years' hard work, have a little more to
live upon than when we first started
(though, indeed, we have very much
more to do with it), look back to the
days long ago, when, in a tiny house,
and with simple furniture, and the
whole world in front of us, domestic
love sweetened every care of life. Are
we so much happier now, when every

half-crown does not want such sharp
looking after, than when we had
seriously to consider if we could afford
a week's holiday, or invite the visit of
a friend? How rich, too, we thought
ourselves then if we had once in three
months a five-pound note to spare and
spend! How we talked over this way
and that of doing the best with it, and
at last picked up something to make
the little drawing-room brighter, or
perhaps bought some second-hand
books for the study shelves. The
enjoyment was so keen because the
pleasure was so rare.

This is also just as true in the question of holidays. Many gentle people
prefer to travel third-class without
being in the least ashamed of it; and
if they are a little more tired at the end
of the day, they have the money in
their pockets which the difference in
the fare has saved. A country farm-
house where you have to keep your
jar of live-bait in the same room where

you eat your meals, and where you share your simple shelter with the dogs of the house, if not with inquisitive chickens, will cost less, but be every whit as enjoyable as the well-furnished villa, with its walled garden and greenhouse, but where, at the end of your stay, you have to pay for every dent in the wall and scratch on the paper, the air no fresher, the country no lovelier, but the rent greater, and the life so much less of a real change.

Besides, a certain scantiness of purse makes the wits strangely nimble in ways of laying out money to the best advantage. You take trouble, you make inquiries, you hunt, and compare, and calculate; and when you have found what you wanted, it seems doubly earned. Majestically to walk into a shop, easily to select the first thing that suits you, always to have money enough to pay for it, never to be compelled to choose what is worse because it is cheaper, no doubt has its

advantages; and who would under-
value them ? But there are real com-
pensations for the multitude, who have
to make an appetite for their food by
first earning it ; and among the simple
and innocent enjoyments of quiet
people, none, perhaps, has more zest
in it, or reward after it, than a long
day's search for some special object,
which they cannot give more than a
certain sum for, and which they know
is to be had if they are not afraid of
trouble.

Besides, there is not only much
happiness to be enjoyed consistently
with the circumstances of what is now
called poverty, there is also much
happiness to be given. The secret of
being well off is to know how to do
without things. The secret of helping
others to be well off is not the mono-
poly of those who can give great
presents or confer big favours ; it is
also with those who can make trifles
go a long way on the errands of kind-

ness, and who can brighten their gifts with love, if they cannot gild them with splendour.

This age is dear for some things, but it is cheap for others. All round, probably, it takes much more to keep a family even in the simplest fashion than a generation ago. But life is much less dull, and shut up, and commonplace, and uninteresting, than it used to be when there were no railways, no cheap press, no penny postage, no lawn-tennis, no Mudie's library. There is more refinement in some homes, if there is more luxury in others; and if meat and rent cost more, clothes and journeys cost less. But all this bears on the possibility of making others happy, limited as our means may be; in the occasions of simple hospitality, in the lending of books and writing of letters, and interchange of trifling and pleasant gifts. No doubt it is delightful to receive a fifty-pound note from a kind grandmother, and to be told you are to do with it just what you please; but sometimes that which costs only five shillings gives just as much pleasure; and a heart that loves to see a child smile may buy as many smiles as it wants for sixpence apiece.

Money also tests character, in the way it indicates and develops the moral disposition, whether for evil or good. Almost the first advice that a kindly man of the world would give to a youth just entering upon it would be, "Never treat money affairs with levity." It has been said of horses that they are noble creatures in themselves, but that somehow they contrive to demoralise all who have much to do with them. It may with equal truth be said of money, that in itself it is a necessary and useful thing; but unless we handle it carefully it will burn our fingers. A professional man, who permits any one but himself to open his letters, had better keep his counsel about it, for cautious clients may not be pleased ; and when a person entrusted with other people's money permits any hand but his own to sign cheques, he runs a risk which it may be hard to justify.

Then every one has some weak point about money, and almost every one is extravagant in some things and penurious in others. A noble nature is noble with money. It is just what one would have expected of gallant King Amadeus, that he should insist on restoring the Escurial out of his own purse. Small-natured people are small with their money, and to get sixpence out of them is like drawing a double tooth. Wasteful people are often stingy; for this is their only way of recouping themselves for their improvidence.

But stingy people are often wasteful, just because they are stingy. A stitch in time saves nine. Timidity often defeats its own purpose. Rome in the

E

end had to pay as much for the three remaining books of the Sibyl as would have bought the six others ; and a little courage in buying is sometimes the truest economy.

It is an inspired maxim, "that he that hateth suretiship is sure" (Proverbs xi. 15). But it does not need inspiration to see that no one should consent to be a trustee for others who is not prepared to take a good deal of trouble, or who is not qualified by the proper experience for fairly doing his best. Money committed to us for a particular purpose should, in the absence of discretionary power, be strictly spent on it, or fresh instructions procured. With certain persons it is a necessary precaution, not only to indicate the way in which your money is to be expended, but to take care that it gets there. Some people have a deep crack running from head to foot through their moral nature. If you send them money for a child's

schooling, it is spent on a silk gown ;
or the cheque that you intended to fill
their coal-cellar is as likely as not to
go for a trinket. Where some people
make their money go much farther
than others do, it is not necessarily
because they are so much more clever,
but because they give their mind to it,
and feel it a duty, as well as a pleasure
to make the most of it. It is almost
always those who have least money
who indulge themselves most, and
those who have most money who
indulge themselves least. Do you
doubt it ? The reason is clear. When
you have something to lose, it is a
matter of importance not to lose it.
If you have nothing to lose, to plunge
a little deeper under water can hurt
no one but the unfortunate tradesman
who gives you credit. In solemn truth,
there can be no kind of doubt that
excessive expenditure of living is one
of the great vices of the time ; and it
would be well for all of us if the power

of the pulpit were more frequently
and vigorously exercised in sternly
discountenancing the selfish thought-
lessness that buys what it cannot pay
for, and in stigmatising a deliberate
and persevering extravagance by its
proper name of fraud.

Yet carefulness about money has
its own dangers. When an Apostle
wrote to the Church of God, " Let your
conversation be without covetousness "
(Heb. xiii. 5), and a Hebrew prophet
ages before him sternly denounced the
then growing habit of adding house to
house and field to field, it was because
then, as much as now, every virtue
has a tendency to deteriorate into a
corresponding vice ; and if to waste
money is a fault, to love it is a sin.
Now it is much easier to come to love
it than some of us may suppose. To
be always worrying about small expenses, or regretting past losses, or
talking about prices, or even comparing
too closely and anxiously one year's

accounts with another's, will secretly,
but inevitably, mildew the spirit with
a kind of sordid earthliness. To give
away will become harder, for we shall
soon fancy we cannot afford it; and
what at first was but a just carefulness
about daily spending, if not watched
against, will presently change even a
liberal man into a miser. Then your
punishment will come in the shape
God sees you to need, and in the
shape you will most dread. Either the
wealth itself will be taken from you,
and the idol of gold will be shattered
before your eyes; or some child or
heir for whom you were destroying
your very soul is taken from you, to
the incorruptible treasure of the better
country; and so the Psalmist's sentence
comes home to you as with the thrust
of the sword point: " He heapeth up
riches, and knoweth not who shall
gather them " (Psalm xxxix 6).

Perhaps there is hardly any sin to
which religious people are more prone

than covetousness; nor any kind of inconsistency which worldly people are more quick to detect, and more severe to denounce ; nor any which a righteous God hates with more perfect hatred, and more inflexibly pursues with His loving chastisement until either it is scourged out of the soul, or the sinner ˙s left to his idols.

The end of it all is this. If money comes, let it come. He who sends it surely does not mean it to hurt us. We need not fear it with a feeble terror, though no one sin has ruined so many souls as covetousness. We will not spring at it with a flutter of excited joy, for it is a grievous trial to the humblest and simplest.

And if money goes, let it go; only let us see that it does not go through folly or sin of ours. Job lost his in one way, and Lot lost his in another. The end of Job was a crown of glory, but the candle of Lot went out in hideous night. Probably there are few

of us who have lived to middle life—
very few indeed who have passed it—
to whose door could be laid no error of
judgment in spending their money, no
taint of conscience in making it. In
this greatest of great trusts, who has
not sometimes failed? Conscience has
said, " Give," and we have not given.
We have steeled our hearts, and sum-
moned our coldest judgment to justify
us in refusals, which now we would
gladly get back; but it is too late.
Witnesses to our self-indulgence sur-
round us in every room we enter. If
we have done something for our Lord,
our heart whispers we might have done
so much more !

But there is time in front; and He
who gives us power to get wealth will
also give us wisdom to use it, if we
really ask Him. Let us be wise,
simple, and kind.

Wise as those who have been called
to liberty, and mean to use it; believ-
ing in God's love to us, understanding

that He intends and expects us to be happy; with a healthy conscience that does not chafe us about every half-penny, yet guided in all we do by the steady purpose of a heart that has been taught to think as in the presence of God.

Simple, so that money shall not spoil us with its influences of power, nor vulgarise us with its tendencies to display, nor coax us with the softness of its luxury. Surely some allowance should be made for rich people as well as for poor. If God, who knows their difficulties, must be ready to bear with them, let us bear; but let us also see how blessed is the lot of those who, being neither rich nor poor, dwell in the temperate zone of a kind of safe table-land, which is neither chilled by want nor swept by tropical storms. Oh, how terrible must death be to a rich man, who has never so used his riches as to have friends to welcome him into the heavenly habitations, and whose only idea of Lazarus, in the other world, is that he should still wait upon him there !

And kind, for " blessed is he that considereth the poor ;" and if every one is poor in something, in which some one else is rich, great are the opportunities of little benevolences, not only from equals to equals, but from one class to another class, whereby but a small amount of money will enable thoughtful hearts to smooth the hard pillow of their suffering kinsmen. There are many and various cups of cold water which tender hands can lift to parched lips with the promised blessing of their divine Redeemer ; many little gifts and many secret offerings which He will publicly recognise in the Great Day. Do we all quite see what is put into our power if our hearts are kind, though our means be scanty ? Do we clearly understand that the true virtue of almsgiving is in being our own almoners ; that the

trifle from our own hand pressed into
hot and thinned fingers with a smile
that gleams with sympathy, and a word
that recalls the sympathy of Christ, is
worth ten times more to man, perhaps
also to God, than a purse of gold sent
through a stranger? Oh, there are so
many ways, if only we cared to think
of them and walk in them, of softening
hardship, and cheering sadness, of lift-
ing off burdens from heavy shoulders,
of making the breaking heart to leap
with joy. If the night is wet, and
times are hard, and my pocket permits
it, no police table of fares shall prevent
my giving a sober cabman half-a-
crown, if I please, instead of a shilling.
Street beggars let no one aid, they are
a cankerous imposthume on English
life; but the thought of one's own
children in comfort at home may well
make the heart tender to boys and girls
who sweep crossings; and no amount
of annual subscriptions to philanthropic
institutions can excuse a Christian man

from personal assistance to the want
that meets him at his own door. To
love, even as we are loved—here is
the effort of earth and the blessedness
of heaven ! No doubt there are many
ways of showing it ; but one way is
money, and God asks for it. " Inas-
much as ye have done it unto one of
the least of these my brethren, ye
have done it unto me " (Matt. xv. 40).